Just The Two Of Us

M Guevarra

notionpress.com

INDIA • SINGAPORE • MALAYSIA

ISBN
Paperback 979-8-89906-591-0
Hardcase 979-8-89961-281-7

To you reading this,

May this book be a companion to your journey, a reminder of love's infinite shapes and the unspoken beauty in every fleeting moment. Thank you for opening these pages; within them lies my heart, laid bare for you to explore.

To you,

You have captured my heart in a way no one else ever could. Your smile, your eyes, and the grace with which you cherish those around you—each of these speaks to a soul so rare and extraordinary. I marvel at the love and values instilled in you, a testament to how beautifully your parents raised you. I find myself lost in a deep sense of admiration.

You are the quiet force behind every thought I pen. This book is a testament to the love you have awakened within me—a love that deepens with every fleeting glance, every cherished moment I hold of you in my heart.

Thank you for being my inspiration, for teaching me the meaning of love in its truest, most genuine form.

With All My Heart,
~M~

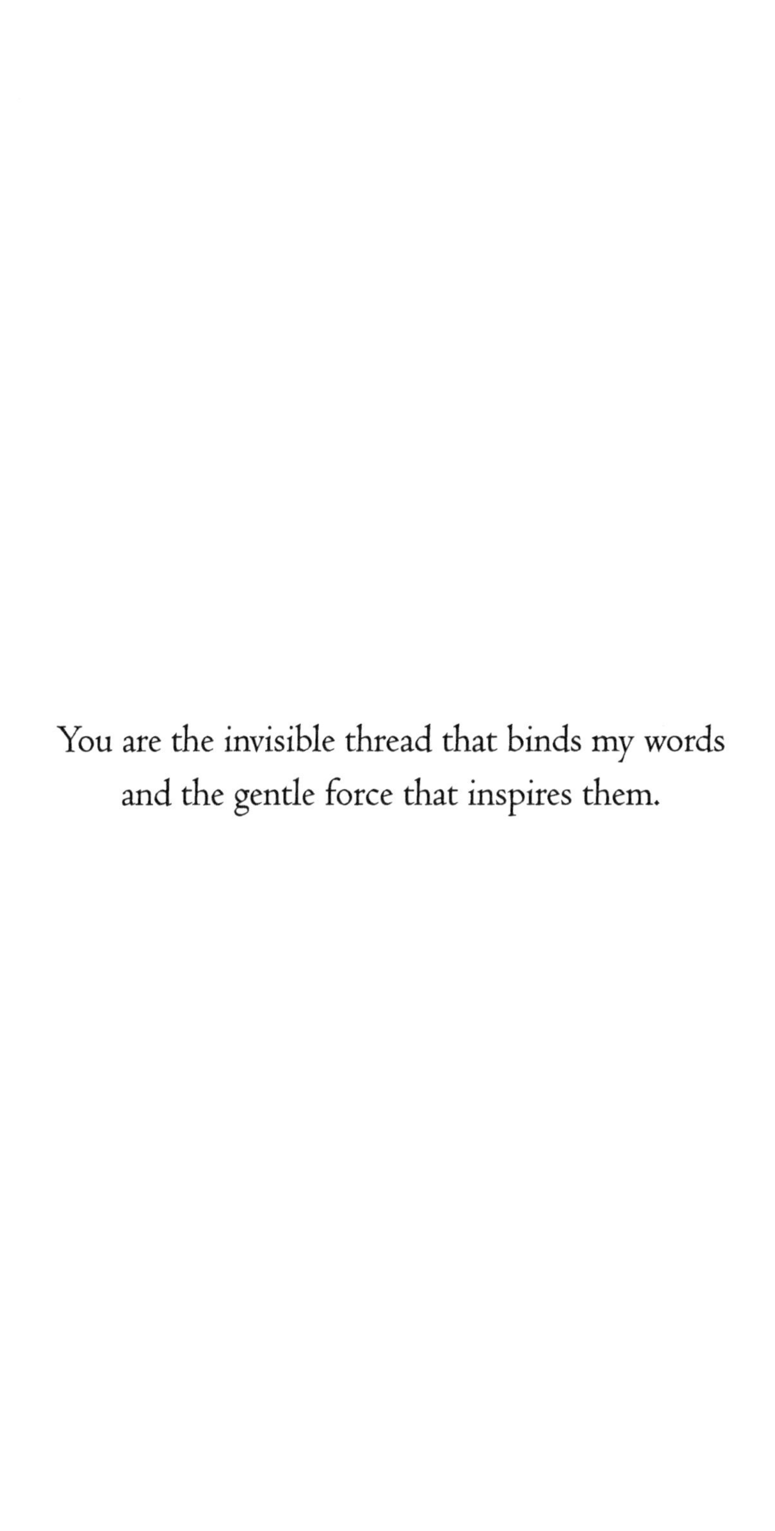

You are the invisible thread that binds my words
and the gentle force that inspires them.

Invisible String

They say that soulmates are destined to find their way back to each other, no matter how far life pulls them apart. And now, as I stand here, lost in the depths of your gaze, I know without a doubt how true that is. We are not here by accident, but by the quiet, deliberate hand of fate, leading us back to one another.

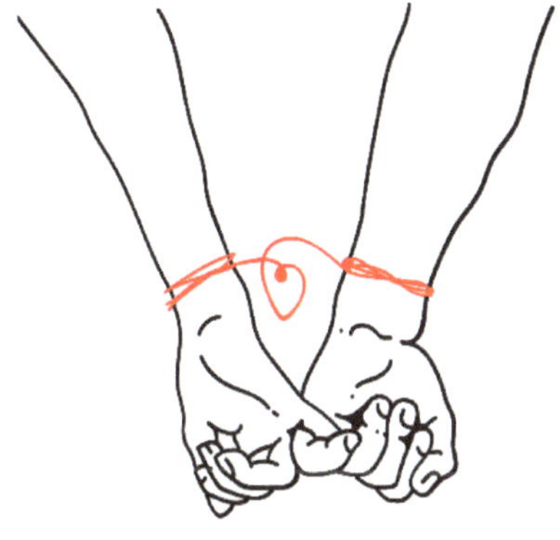

In this moment, as we exchange promises that will ripple through time, I feel the weight of every challenge we've overcome dissolve, and the warmth of every future joy draws nearer. It's as if the universe itself orchestrated our reunion, weaving together two hearts that beat as one, crafting a love story that transcends a lifetime — an eternal bond, forever sealed.

I choose you, and I will choose you every single day.

My Dearest,

You've shown me something I never imagined I would need. For the longest time, I believed I had to discover myself in isolation, to wander through life searching for meaning on my own. But that belief was wrong — so utterly wrong. You have illuminated my path in ways I didn't think possible, and through you, I've uncovered my truest self.

Before you, I thought the journey of understanding who I am was a solitary one. But then you came into my life, and everything changed. In your presence, I discovered not just who I am, but who I am meant to be. You've brought out parts of me that I never knew existed. Through your love, I've found purpose, something deeper than words can explain. You are my mirror, reflecting the best parts of me, the parts I didn't even know were there.

Every moment with you has been a revelation, a reminder of why life is beautiful. You've awakened in me a sense of belonging, a feeling that there is more to this world than wandering alone. With you, I have not only found my path, but I've realized that my purpose was never about just finding myself — it was about finding you.

In loving you, I have found my reason for being, and that is more precious than anything I could have ever dreamed of.

Yours always.

Always

From the day you came in,
Like the dawn, quiet and sure,
You carved your place within.

In the silent corners of my soul,
Where only you could see,
You've lit a flame that time can't dim,
A bond that will always be.

From now until the stars grow cold,
Through whispers, winds and rain,
You'll rest in me, a part of life,
In joy, in love, in pain.

For in here always,
You've become my endless song,
From the day you came until forever.

My home, my last train, my end game – it's you, and it will always be you. I'm taking you, body and soul, into every moment that follows. No matter where life leads, my heart finds its way back to you.

I love you, and I'm sure of you – through every season of life…

Falling in a Blink

I still remember the day you walked past me. It was as if the world slowed down for just a moment. Your sweet scent lingered in the air, pulling me in, while your eyes—so bright, so full of life— seemed to capture all the light in the room. There was a glow around you, a radiance that made everything else fade into the background. It struck me so deeply, I didn't even realize I was holding my breath, but I knew in that instant I couldn't forget you, even if I tried. It only took a second—just one—for me to fall completely, irreversibly in love with you.

Unwritten Truths

Your name had been etched in my heart long before I even realized that you were the one I had been searching for all along. I was terrified to acknowledge it, but you've transformed every part of me. You bring out my deepest truths and unveil my vulnerabilities in a way no one else can...

My Dearest,

To win your heart, I've come to understand, it's not a matter of grand gestures or loud declarations. Your heart is far too deep, far too wise for such fleeting displays. What you desire, what your soul craves, is something lasting, something true. I realize now that to love you is to learn you — to see beyond your beauty, as captivating as it is, and to discover the depth within, the stories you don't always speak, the tenderness in your silence.

I want to know the rhythm of your world, to notice the little things that make you smile, the moments that brighten your spirit. I want to be patient with you, to take my time, not to rush toward some imagined goal but to simply be there, beside you, in every moment, both the shining ones and the quiet, everyday spaces where life truly happens. I want you to know that I am here — not with any expectations or demands, but with the pure desire to be the person you can trust, the one you can lean on, without ever feeling weighed down by obligation.

Your honesty, your authenticity, these are what draw me in, and I want to be real with you. I want to share my thoughts, my dreams, even the parts of me I'm not always proud of. I want you to see all of me, because in you I see someone who values truth over appearances, consistency over mere flash. And I want you to know that what you see in me is sincere, that my intentions are as steady as they are genuine.

I want to show you kindness, not just in how I treat you, but in how I live my life. I know how deeply you notice the way people move through the world, and I want my actions to speak for me where words sometimes fall short. I want you to see that in my kindness, there is love, and in my patience, there is devotion.

And over time, I hope you will see that you no longer have to guard yourself from me, that the walls you've built can come down. I won't chase you; I'll walk alongside you, as slowly as you need, with trust, with respect, and with a love that grows quietly, steadily, and without fear.

Yours, always and patiently.

If you could look into my heart, you'd see how I fall deeper in love with you every single day.

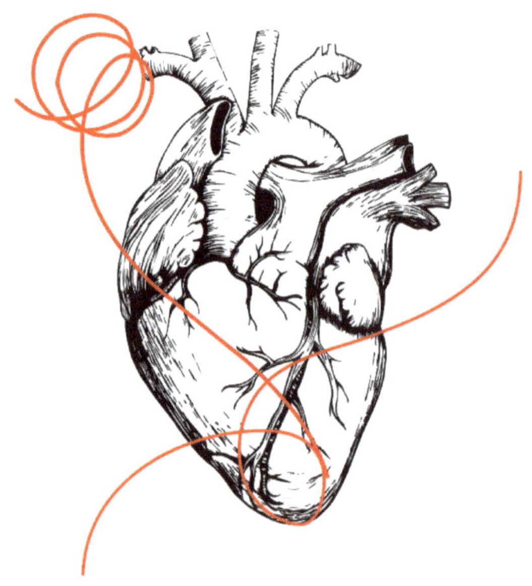

"*You are the dream that whispers through my sleepless nights,*
A miracle that anchors my faith in the extraordinary,
And a fantasy long cherished,
Awaiting to unfold into reality,
Where our hearts entwine like poetry, etched in the stars."

Awakened

The world I once lived in was black and white—a place where the colors of life felt muted, distant, and unreachable. Each day blurred into the next moments passing by without meaning, and joy seemed like a foreign concept I had long forgotten. Then you appeared—a ray of sunshine breaking through the gloom. Your radiant smile illuminated every dark corner of my heart. It wasn't just any smile; it was yours—the kind that brought warmth and light to a place I believed could never be reached again. In that moment, everything changed.

For the first time in what felt like an eternity, I began to grasp what genuine happiness could feel like. It wasn't grand or overwhelming—it was soft, subtle, and infinitely powerful. I could write thousands of words to describe you—how your presence transformed my world, how your kindness breathed new life into me—but even then, words would fall short. There is depth to this feeling that transcends language, a brightness you bring that can't be contained in phrases.

What I know for sure is that life, with all its shades and colors, is no longer something I merely observe. It's something I feel, deeply, because of you – because you chose to light up my world.

In your presence, the pieces of my heart find their place, and for the first time, I feel whole.

Let's Get Lost Through a Lifetime

I want to see the world with you—not just through the usual lenses of adventure or discovery, but through the soft glow of our shared moments. With you, every landscape becomes a masterpiece, every city holds a secret waiting for us to unravel. I imagine walking down unknown streets, where the hum of life is unfamiliar, yet your presence makes it all feel like home.

The world seems vast, but when we're together, it shrinks into something intimate—just you, me, and the horizon we chase. The colors of each sunrise are brighter, not because they've changed, but because I see them reflected in your eyes. I want to feel the pulse of distant lands and the rhythm of foreign seas, knowing that each step, each breath, is one we share.

We'll get lost, not in maps, but in the thrill of discovering the world in ways only we can—through laughter, quiet looks, and the simple joy of being together. The world is beautiful, but with you, it becomes infinite.

"Your eyes speak volumes, a thousand whispered tales,
Hands that soothe storms with a gentle grace.
And a love destined to remain timeless, never fading
with age."

If doubt creeps in, know that my eyes tell the truth of how I feel about you. And I will always stay true with all the words I say to you…

My Dearest,

There are words we speak to each other every day, but none of them seem enough to capture the depth of what I feel for you. Even as I write this, I wonder if I can truly express the quiet, constant pull you have in my heart. But still, I must try.

When I look at you, I see more than just your beauty; I see a future, a comfort, a sense of belonging that I've never known before. Your presence has become my peace, your voice — my comfort. In every shared glance, I find a certainty that I've rarely found in life, and that certainty is this: **I love you, deeply and without hesitation.**

There are times when words fail me, when I'm standing beside you, and the weight of how much you mean to me renders me speechless. But even in those moments, I hope you feel it — the love I carry for you in my heart. It's not loud or boastful; it's quiet, steadfast, the kind that stays even in the moments of silence.

If ever there is a shadow of doubt in your heart, I want you to remember this; I am yours — fully, completely, and without reservation. My love for you is not just in the words I say, but in the way I'll always stand beside you, the way I'll reach for your hand without thinking, and the way I'll listen when you need to talk. It's in the way I'll always choose you, every day, no matter what.

So, if the world feels uncertain, or if we face storms ahead, know that my love is the one thing that will never waver. I will always be here, true to you, true to us – with all my heart.

Just The Two of Us.

It's You—Only You

You've shown me what it truly means to love and to be loved in return. With you, I no longer fear lowering my guard. When I'm with you, there's a tenderness that makes me feel safe, as if nothing else matters but us. I can be completely open, and you hold my vulnerability with such care, as though it's something precious.

How Do You Do That?

How do you make me fall deeper in love with you every single day? Effortlessly, you make my heart race, as if it's about to leap from my chest. Never have I seen heaven so close as I do in your presence…

Love,

I have seen so many beautiful faces, but none compared to yours. There's something about the way you carry yourself, the way your eyes speak a thousand words even when you say nothing at all. It's as if your presence was woven into my soul long before we ever met. The world is full of fleeting beauty, but yours is the one I always come back to, the one that lingers in my thoughts when the day fades into night.

I know I may not be the first to admire you, to hold your attention, or to capture your heart. But what I offer you is more than admiration — it's a promise. I will work every day to be the last one who stands beside you, to be the one who learns every layer of who you are, who sees your strength and your vulnerability, and loves you more for both. I want to be the one who fights for us, who never takes you for granted, and who cherishes the privilege of being by your side.

In a world where people come and go, I want to be your constant. I may not be perfect, but I will give you all of me — my best, my heart, my loyalty. For you, I am willing to grow, to become the person who deserves to be with you, because you are worth every effort.

While I may not be your first, I dream of being your last. The one you turn to, the one who gets to hold your hand through all the seasons of life. Together, I hope we can build a love that endures, a story that no one else can write — but only us.

Yours always in all walks of life.

No Place But Here

I find pieces of you in everything I love, and I love you in every part of me. Being with you feels like holding hands with destiny—knowing that every step we take, whether small or grand, is part of a journey only we can truly understand.

More than anything, I hope you know I am here completely and endlessly for you. My heart beats in rhythm with yours, and with every breath, I'm reminded there's no place I'd rather be than by your side.

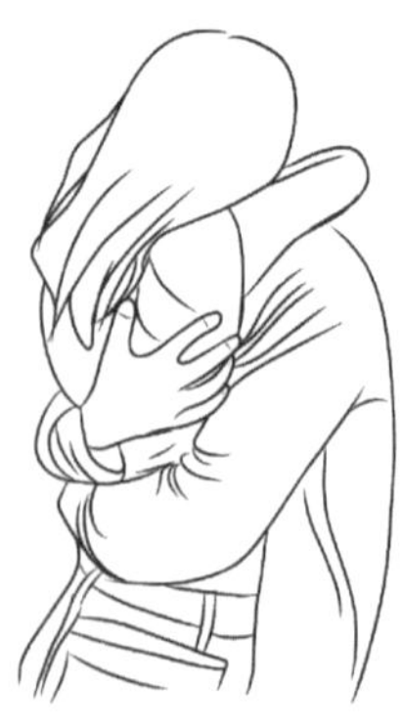

Selfish

Yes, I am. Especially when it comes to you. I don't want to share you, not even with the wind that brushes your skin or the sun that casts its light on you. I want all of you – every breath, every glance, every thought – wrapped around me like a secret, like something only I could ever know. When you're near, it's as though the world fades and all that matters is the space between us. It's not just desire; it's a hunger, a need to keep you close, to make sure that every part of you belongs to me, and just me alone.

The First Note

Do you remember? It was a night wrapped in the warmth of flickering candles and the soft murmur of conversations. You sat there with your guitar, the soft wood gleaming under the gentle glow of the light. As your fingers danced over the strings, an electric hush fell over the room, each pluck resonating in the air, drawing us closer.

The moment you began to sing, it was as if the world around us faded. Your voice, rich and melodic, wrapped around my heart like a tender embrace. The words you uttered were not just lyrics; they felt like secrets whispered into the depths of my soul. Each note you sang set my heart racing, a rhythm I could not ignore.

In that moment, everything changed. I found myself captivated, lost in the cadence of your song and the sincerity in your eyes. It was more than just a performance; it was a connection, a spark igniting something deep within me. You didn't just sing; you told a story, one that I yearned to be a part of.

I remember thinking that I could listen to you forever, each song a new chapter, each word a step deeper into the world you were creating. As the final note lingered in the air, I knew that nothing would ever feel the same. Your music had not only captivated my senses it had woven itself into the very fabric of my being.

I am pouring my thoughts onto the page, compelled to capture the essence of what you mean to me. Each word feels like brushstroke, painting a vivid picture of emotions that are too deep to articulate fully.

The Place I Call Home

From the very start, I loved you—not just for your laughter that dances in the air or the way your eyes light up with unspoken dreams, but for the quiet strength that grounds us both. In your presence, I found solace—a sense of belonging I had never known before…

Confession

I've never been good at speaking my heart, especially when it's tangled with feelings I barely understand. But you make it impossible to keep these emotions quiet, no matter how much I try.

It's in the way you move, with a quiet grace that feels more like poetry in motion than mere steps. There's something captivating in your eyes, as if they hold a thousand stories, each one more intriguing than the last. When you speak, it's as if the world pauses to listen, not because you're loud or commands attention, but because your presence alone demands it in the gentlest way.

You're not like anyone I've known. There's a strength in you, but it's subtle, woven into your smile, your laughter, the way you face the world without ever needing to prove a thing. You exist without effort, without force and yet somehow, you have taken up all the space in my mind. It's the small things too – the way your hair falls over your face when you're focused, the soft hum of your voice when you're thinking, the moments when you let your guard down, and I catch a glimpse of something deeper, something raw and unguarded.

I've watched you from a distance, always too afraid to step closer, terrified of ruining the delicate balance between us. But I can't keep this to myself any longer. I admire you – no more than that, I'm drawn to you in a way that feels inevitable, like I've been walking toward you my whole life without realizing it. Every day I spend near you, I'm reminded that there's something more here, something I've never felt with anyone else…

Even in the mundane moments — when we share silence, or when our laughter echoes against the backdrop of everyday life — I feel a connection that transcends words. I want to tell you how you inspire me to see beauty in the ordinary and how your kindness leaves an indelible mark on my heart.

Gravity of You

That bare face and brown eyes make me fall harder with each glance, like a pull I can't resist. There's something raw, something real in the simplicity of it all—no need for masks or pretenses. Just you, as you are, drawing me deeper, like gravity itself. Every time I look, I find myself sinking into that gaze, as if the whole world falls away, and all that remains is you.

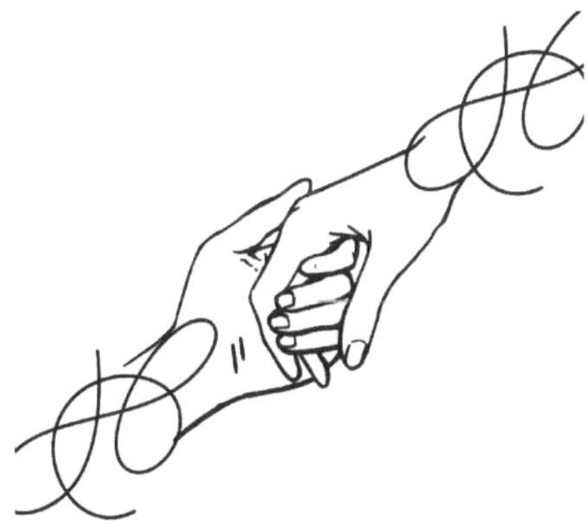

In Every Lifetime

I will be yours through every sunset, through every challenge, through every quiet and chaotic moment. My love, my heart, my very being belongs to you, and I will love you as fiercely as I do now until the end of my days.

My Dearest,

Every moment I spend thinking of you feels like a pause in time, a serene oasis amidst the chaos of the world. I've tried endlessly to capture in words what you mean to me, but language often feels like too small a vessel for the depth of my feelings.

When I'm near you, everything feels right. It's as if your presence fills the gaps in my soul I didn't even know existed. Your smile is a quiet sunrise, illuminating my darkest hours, and your laughter — how it sings to me — is like a melody that echoes in my heart long after the sound has faded.

I am in awe of your strength, your grace, and the way you move through life, shaping it with kindness and resilience. The way you care, not just for me, but for the world around you, are a testament to the beauty of your soul. *With you, I feel safe, like no matter what storms may come, we can weather them together.*

Forever yours.

Glad You Existed

I thank your parents for bringing you into this world, for shaping the person you've become, and for every choice that led you here. I thank the universe for aligning the stars just right, allowing our paths to cross in this vast, unpredictable world, among the millions we could have walked. There are no promises that this will be simple, but I choose it. I choose us — through the laughter and the tears, the moments of joy and the storms of uncertainty. When things are raw and unpolished, I will still be here. Through every high, every low, and even in the moments that feel broken — I'll stay.

The Promise

For you are my constant in this ever – changing world, and I will remain, heart wide open, through the good, the bad, and all the shades in between.

Home

To the one with whom I can share quiet moments over coffee, where every sip feels like a conversation between our souls. To the one who sits with me in a parked car, where the world outside fades, and we dive deep into the kind of therapy only two hearts in sync can provide. Falling in love with you is like finding a home in the simplest of moments – a warm cup in hand, the hum of an engine, and the unspoken understanding that we are exactly where we're meant to be. I'm waiting for that day when we can spend more time together, where those fleeting moments become endless hours, and we can finally bask in the love we've both been waiting for.

I can't name it, and maybe I don't need to. But I know this — being around you makes everything brighter, sharper, more alive. And I think… no, I'm certain — I don't just admire you. I care for you, more deeply than I ever thought possible.

Have You Ever Been in Love?

I find myself asking this question more often than I'd like to admit. It lingers on my lips, dances in my thoughts, and surfaces during quiet moments when the world fades away. Love has a way of wrapping itself around you, squeezing tight and refusing to let go. It's exhilarating and terrifying all at once.

I think I have. It crept up on me like a soft breeze on a warm day, subtle yet undeniable. One moment, I was comfortably wrapped in my solitude, and the next, there you are. Your laughter filled the air, a song that echoed in the corners of my mind. It was in the ways you spoke, with passion and purpose, as if every word was painted on the canvas of your dreams.

Every shared glanced felt electric, a spark igniting an uncharted territory in my heart. I found myself tracing the lines of your smile, memorizing the way your eyes lit up with mischief. There were moments when our fingers brushed together, and the world melted away, leaving only the two of us in a bubble of fleeting eternity. It was intoxicating, like sipping the sweetest wine.

So, have you been in love? If you have, you'll know that it's a journey, a winding road with peaks of joy and valleys of doubt. But even in the most difficult moments, the heart yearns for connection, for the warmth of another. And perhaps, just perhaps, that's what makes it all worthwhile – the hope that love, in all its forms, will always find a way to light up the darkest corners of our existence.

Only One

And if one day, I forget all these, know that the memories are imprinted in my heart, beyond the grasp of time's erosion. Even if my mind surrenders to the fog of forgetfulness, the essence of what we shared remains untouched, like silent, steady pulse within me.

Sunday 1:27 AM

Right here at this moment. The longing, the sadness, and the missing piece I was looking for fade away as I hold you close. I never thought that all this time, the love I was searching for has always been right in front of me — my best friend and my lover in one. I loved you long before my heart realized it.

As much as I tried to deny it, I think I knew from the start that it was you that I needed.

The Soft Glow

Every laugh, every stolen glance, and every tear is etched deep, not in fleeting thoughts but in the very fiber of my soul. If the colors of our past blur and words escape me, understand that the warmth of you still lingers, glowing softly, eternal. Even in silence, I carry you – tenderly, fiercely, forever intertwined with my being.

Just Maybe

I still remember the first time I saw your face. In a split second, you had me saying, "Maybe we could be a thing." It was a crowded café, sunlight streaming through the window, casting golden hues across the room. You were sitting there, lost in thought, a soft smile playing on your lips as you flipped through the pages of a book.

There was something magnetic about you, an energy that drew me in like a moth to a flame. My heart raced as I watched you, the world around us fading into a blur. The sounds of chatter and clinking cups faded, leaving only the steady rhythm of my pulse echoing in my ears.

I imagined us sharing laughter over coffee, our fingers brushing as we reached for the same pastry. I pictured late-night talks under starlit skies, our dreams intertwining like the vines in the garden I had always wanted to cultivate. With every passing moment, my mind spun a tapestry of possibilities, each thread vibrant and alive with potential.

But in that fleeting moment, as I hesitated on the brink of stepping into your world. I wondered if you felt the same spark. Did you sense the invisible tether that seemed to bind us, pulling me closer with every heartbeat?

As I finally gathered the courage to approach you, my heart danced with anticipation and fear. Would you smile and say yes? Or would the magic of that moment dissolve like morning mist, leaving only the bittersweet taste of what might have been?

"Maybe we could be a thing," I whispered under my breath, wishing for the universe to conspire in our favor. The potential hung heavy in the air, and in that instant, I knew I would always remember the way your eyes lit up when you finally met mine.

Though I may not have the eloquence of a seasoned writer, my heart spills onto the page, urging me to express the love that has woven itself into the very fabric of my being. With each line, I hope to convey not just my affection, but a promise – to cherish you, to stand by you, and to celebrate the beautiful journey we share together.

Through Your Eyes

You see parts of me I've never shared before, and instead of turning away, you pull me closer. You don't just love the easy parts—you embrace the messiness, the flaws—and somehow, that makes me fall for you even more.

My Dearest,

I find myself at a loss for words when it comes to describing what you mean to me. It's not just that you are beautiful — though you are, in ways that leave me breathless — but it's the way your presence feels like a quiet solace in a world that moves too fast. You have this grace, this warmth, that reaches out even when you're silent, and it pulls me in, like the tide drawn to the moon.

I think of you often, in moments both big and small. In the stillness of the morning, when the sun rises and the world is awash in a soft glow, it reminds me of how you illuminate my days. In those fleeting seconds when everything is calm, I find my thoughts returning to you, as though your ever essence has woven itself into the fabric of my mind.

There is something about you that inspires me to be more than I am. You don't demand it — there's no need for you to say a word — but simply being in your presence makes me want to be better. It's as if you've shown me what life could be like when shared with someone who sees beyond the surface, who understands the soul.

If I could, I will hold these moments with you in my hands, like delicate treasures, guarding them against the chaos of time. But I know better; I know that what we share is not something to be kept hidden away. It's something to be nurtured, to be honored with every thought, every action and every word I speak.

Always,

~M~

Timeless Connection

And now, I'm holding your hands, feeling the warmth of your skin, a softness that seems to melt into mine. Our fingers interlace as if they've always known the way to each other. I look into your eyes, those deep wells of calm and light, and I lose track of time, as if the world has slowed just for us. My hand gently caresses your face, tracing the delicate lines of your cheek, your jaw, memorizing every curve. In this moment, everything else fades. There is no past, no future – only the quiet rhythm of our breaths and the unspoken promise between us.

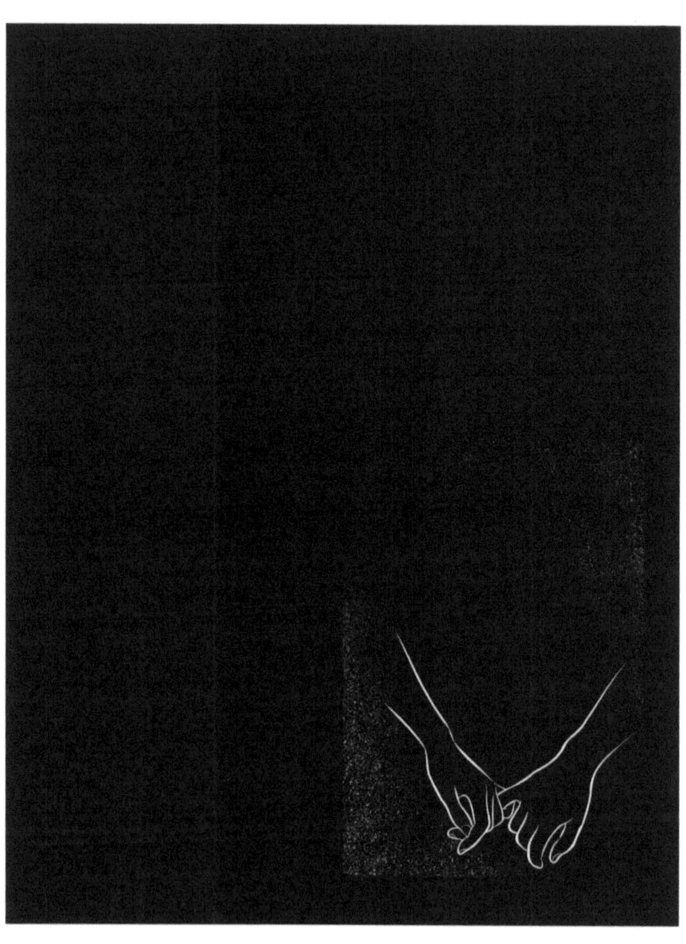

Stay

Promise me you'll stay, even when the sky darkens, and the storm settles heavy in our hearts. Stay when the days feel long and the nights even longer, when silence wraps around us like a cold, unfamiliar embrace. Stay when the weight of the world presses down on our spirits and giving up feels like the easiest path.

Monday 2:59 AM

Even when it hurts, even when it's hard, promise me you won't let go. Because I won't.

Question?

How could I ever choose anyone else but you, my love? In your presence, the world melts away, leaving only us in this tender embrace. You are my solace in a chaotic world, the melody that soothes my soul. Each moment with you is a treasure, a sweet reminder of how love can blossom in — so here I stand, forever captivated by you, lost in a dream that feels like reality, yearning to cherish you for all the days to come.

Unspoken "What-ifs"

But love isn't just the beautiful moments; it's the vulnerability that comes with it. It's the fear of baring your souls, of letting someone see you in your rawest form. There were nights when doubt seeped in, whispering shadows of insecurity to me. What if I'm not enough? What if you see the flaws I hide so carefully?

Weathering The Storm with You

Hold on when the laughter fades, when the warmth of the good times seems distant, and the future feels uncertain. Stay, even then, when doubt creeps in, whispering that it might be simpler to walk away. Promise me that when the road gets rough, when we're stumbling through the unknown, you'll stand beside me. We'll push through the dark, together…

"I didn't know love
Until I looked at your face.
It's the most precious thing I've ever seen,
Worth keeping
And worth loving."

Sanctuary

Yet, amidst the uncertainty, I learned that love is also about acceptance. It's the way you listened—truly listened—to my stories, my fears, my dreams. You embraced the chaos of my mind, and in turn, I found peace in your presence. Love becomes a sanctuary where imperfections are celebrated, where two souls entwine in a dance of understanding.

Saturday, 5:24 AM

I've been sitting here, staring at the moon, watching as it bows gracefully to the sun. In the stillness of the night, I can feel the weight of its gentle farewell, the way it softens into the horizon, much like the quiet moments before I see you. The moon, with its soft glow, is a reminder of your presence even in the dark, constant and unwavering. But then, the sun – bold and radiant – rises, and in its warmth, I find the fire you spark in me.

Together, they create this perfect balance, like you and me, day and night, light and shadow, always chasing each other, always belonging.

Where My Heart Find Rest

No matter how many storms I weather or how weary my heart becomes, I belong to you—always and forever. You are my constant, my peace, the unwavering anchor that keeps me grounded. And though exhaustion may come and go, my love for you is boundless, eternal, and untouched by time.

Safe Haven

I'm tired—my body aches, my mind weighs heavy with the burdens of the day—but I will never grow tired of you. You are the calm amidst my demons, the light that softens my shadows. In your presence, I find comfort that words cannot fully capture. You are my sanctuary, my safe zone, the place where I am wholly myself, free and unguarded.

Labyrinth

And then, like dawn breaking over a long, dark night, I saw you clearly – your burst of mirth like music, your eyes holding galaxies of dreams and untold stories. In that moment, the fragments of my heart came together, and the world shifted into focus. I understood that the quest had not been for something outside myself, but for the recognition of what had always been there, patiently waiting.

"Fall deeply,
Love sincerely,
Until you find that love,
That last a lifetime of memories."

Just the Two of Us

I didn't know that I could fall harder than before, that my heart still had the capacity for this kind of surrender. I was caught in a cycle of losing and gaining, endlessly shifting between what I had and what was slipping through my fingers. I had learned to move through life as if it were a game, my steps calculated, my emotions guarded, winning some battles but always feeling the weight of what I lost.

Until I found you.

Suddenly, the rules changed. It wasn't a game anymore — it was real, raw and undeniable. The walls I built so carefully began to crumble, and with you, it was different. Falling didn't feel like defeat but like the most natural thing, like discovering I could fly in the very act of letting go. What I thought was a loss transformed into something far richer, more profound — a connection that felt like a gain beyond measure.

With you, I wasn't afraid of falling. I was free to embrace the descent, because with you, it felt like I was finally landing home.

Infinitely Falling

As I sink deeper into this silent embrace, a ghost of the past fades without a trace. For in this fall, I've discovered my flight – with you, every moment becomes pure delight. A feather adrift on love's open shores, through the storms and through the rain – through the joy and even in pain. In this boundless journey, I will always remain – forever yours.

Dancing in Imperfection

In the dim light of the room, you step onto the floor, a blend of hesitance and hope. Your shy smile blooms like a fragile flower, radiating warmth amidst the uncertainty. As the music begins to swell, I can't help but watch as you sway, each movement a story whispered between beats.

Your steps are awkward yet enchanting, a rhythm that doesn't quite fit the melody. You stumble, and in that moment, my heart races — not from the fear of the fall, but from the sheer beauty of your authenticity. It's in those imperfect moments that I find myself captivated, drawn to you.

I laugh softly when your foot finds mine, a gentle bruise that becomes a mark of joy rather than pain. It's a reminder of our shared rhythm, the beauty of our imperfect choreography. I love every piece of you – the shy smile, the hesitant steps, the way you let go just a little more with each passing note.

We dance like two clumsy souls lost in the music, and I don't care about the missteps. With every twist and turn, I discover a deeper affection for your flaws, those quirks that make you wholly you. The laughter we share becomes the sweetest refrain, echoing in the corners of my heart.

Let us dance, you and I, in this world of imperfections. Let me hold your hand and guide you through the rhythm of our unrefined steps.

Letter to Heaven

I wrote a letter to heaven, asking God to keep you safe while you find your way to me. Until then, I'll work on myself to become a better version of me, so that when we finally cross paths, we will both be ready for the love and life we are destined to share.

And then you came—like a hush before a storm, unexpected and beautiful. Your laughter stirred the stillness I'd grown used to, and something within me awakened.

I wasn't ready—but you made the world feel lighter.

Then fear crept in. What if I lost you? Love, I realized, wasn't just joy—it was risk. But even in fear, I kept writing. Each word a quiet promise – I may be finding my way, but my heart already knows its home—in you.

To love you feels like standing before the dawn — soft, radiant, and full of promise. You are the kind of beauty that don't merely admire; you are someone to cherish — with a love that grows stronger, like a rose blooming with each passing moment.

Written in the Stars

I don't know how to explain how deeply I care for you, except to say that you've become a part of my world in a way that feels effortless, natural—like we were meant to meet, meant to feel this. And if you'll let me, I'll spend each day showing you what it means to be loved, not just through words, but in the quiet moments in between, where real love grows.

I am neither a writer nor a poet, yet I could fill pages with words about you. Still, no amount of ink could ever truly capture the depth of what my heart feels for you.

With you, I don't need to hide. You make me feel like I can be completely myself, and that's enough. I've never felt so free, so deeply connected. With you, I have found not only a partner but a haven.

Your eyes, clear and expressive, hold mysteries only the heart could hope to unravel, and with a glance, they stir something deep within — a longing, a quite affection, a sense of wonder.

Caught in the Moment

You are a whisper in a loud world, a presence that fills the room with subtle elegance. And I am caught in your orbit, finding myself unable to look away, as if your very essence is woven into the air I breathe.

Radiance in the Quiet

As you stand like a quiet bloom amidst the chaos, your beauty is soft and undeniable—like a rose capturing every gaze with its perfect symmetry. Your skin glows with a natural light, radiating warmth and calm, as if your presence alone could soothe even the roughest days.

You are my reminder that, even in the most turbulent moments, there is always something gentle that can restore balance.

My Day One

Remember the first time we kissed? It was a moment suspended in time, the world around us fading into a soft blur. Your lips – yes, your lips – were the sweetest I have ever tasted, like honey melting on my tongue. I had kissed a few back then, fleeting encounters that left little more than a whisper of memory. But you? You were different.

I want to thank your ex. Sometimes, it's strange how life works out. What one person lets go of has become my treasure, and in that bittersweet truth, I see the beauty of fate.

Tuesday, 5:00 AM

As I took each step forward, I found that love was less about readiness and more about the willingness to embrace the journey, with all its uncertainties. I would cherish our moments, no matter how brief, and learn to let go of the fear that tried to keep me from fully loving you.

I know I may not be great with spoken words, but
here I am, pouring my heart onto the page — bleeding
through every sentence, letting the world see just how
incredibly lucky I am to be in love with you, and even
luckier to be loved by you in return.

In Every Season

Where the world may drain me, you fill me with a warmth that never fades. Your smile, your touch, the way your voice dances through the air—these things revive me. The more I give, the more I am replenished, for you are a wellspring that never runs dry.

The world spins on, relentless in its demands, and yet, here I am—tired, drained, yearning for a moment of peace. I could surrender to the quiet, give in to the desire to rest, but there is one thing I know for certain – I *will never get tired of you.*

Inked

Words spill from me, barely contained, driven by an admiration I can't quite put into words. I may not have the skill of seasoned writers or the elegance of poets, but the depth of what I feel pushes me to try. I want to capture even a little bit of your beauty and grace.

Every word I write, every thought I share, is my attempt to show you the impact you've had on me. Your presence lights something inside me, sparking feelings of wonder and affection that I sometimes struggle to express. When I try to describe your loveliness, I realize how small language feels, how impossible it is to truly capture the warmth and light you bring into my life.

Yet, despite the limitations of my expression, I am driven by a sincere desire to convey just a fraction of what you mean to me. Through these imperfect attempts, I hope to give you a glimpse of the admiration that overwhelms me, the way you have touched my heart, and the profound effect it had on my world.

~M~

Every glance, every smile, every word you speak draws me closer, fueling my yearning to know you more intimately.

Timeless

You have shown me that to love is to embrace my own flaws, to fill my heart with courage and hope. And from this day onward, I will walk beside you through all the seasons of our lives— through the darkest nights and the stormiest days, with you, always.

"Love will always find its way,
To people who are ready to get hurt and be
loved at the same time.
It may never be the kind of love you dreamed about,
But a love that will make you,
The best version of yourself…"

Always, Ours

The beauty of you and me is that it's not limited to moments, but rather an enduring presence. It is the quiet assurance that no matter where life takes us, no matter how far we might go, we will always have this space that belongs solely to us — two souls, forever intertwined.

"I want to paint picture of you,
But I can't.
All I can do,
Is to stare at your beauty.

Memorize the curve of your lips,
The perfect shape of your body.
And the color of your skin.

Even when I close my eyes,
It's always you that I see.
And a picture that I could keep,
Forever in my heart."

My Dearest,

In a world full of noise and distractions, I've discovered something truly special——our connection, the moments when it's simply just the two of us. When everything else falls away, it's in those quiet spaces between us that I find the most comfort. In your presence, I am at peace. There's a unique kind of magic in the way we don't need many words to understand each other — we simply know.

This bond we share is more than just being physically together. It's the deep understanding between us, the unspoken language that exists beyond time or place. It's in the way we smile at each other, how a touch says everything we need, how laughter flows easily over the simplest of things. With you, I've found a sense of belonging that feels effortless and true—a certainty that the world aligns perfectly when we are side by side.

Amid the chaos of life, I find tranquility in the simplicity of our connection. Whether we're talking for hours, gazing at the stars, or simply sharing a silent moment, it doesn't matter. What matters is that we're together, creating a world of our own, where love becomes stronger with every passing day.

It's not about the moments we share but the enduring presence of what we've built. No matter where life takes us, we'll always have this space, a space that is ours alone. It's a place where our love flourishes, where everything feels possible because we face it together.

I love you not just for who you are, but for how you make me feel when we're together. You are my heart, my home, my forever.

With all my love,

~M~

"All it takes is one brave step to turn friends into lovers—and once taken, nothing is ever the same."

And now, in the silence between us, I tremble——not because I don't want more, but because I fear losing what we already are.